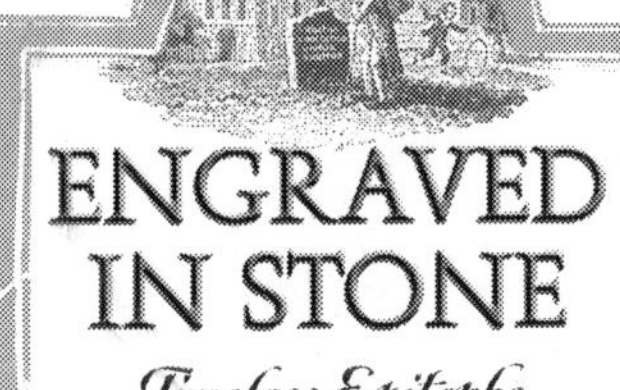

ENGRAVED IN STONE

Timeless Epitaphs of Celebrities, Scoundrels and Everyday People

COMPILED BY JO ERICKSON

ENGRAVED IN STONE:
Timeless Epitaphs of Celebrities, Scoundrels and Everyday People

Design, editorial and production by
Matthews Communications Design Inc.

Library and Archives Canada Cataloguing in Publication

Erickson, Jo

Engraved in stone : timeless epitaphs of celebrities, scoundrels and everyday people / compiled by Jo Erickson.

ISBN 0-9736108-0-8

1. Epitaphs. I. Title.
PN6291.E75 2004 929'.5 C2004-904373-0

Published by MCD Books
An imprint of Matthews Communications Design Inc.
www.matthewscommdesign.com

Printed in Canada

1234567 FNIS 07 06 05 04

Contents

To the volunteers
of hospice care
everywhere

FOREWORD

To give care and comfort to the dying is important work. It is the kind of work that defines our essential humanity. So a book of epitaphs – many of them flippant and humorous – might seem like an odd, some might say disrespectful, way to pay tribute to those who are both the agents and beneficiaries of hospice care.

Yet death is the one unavoidable reality. It is the endpoint at which our lives achieve a final perspective. And epitaphs, I believe, are simply an expression of this. They are ultimately celebratory and life-affirming.

So I hope that, in reading this book, you'll find time to pause (with the occasional smile), and consider the wonderful legacy of those who have left us.

On behalf of those involved in hospice care (which will be receiving a portion of the proceeds from the sale of this book), I thank you for your support.

Jo Erickson
Uxbridge, 2004

I

UNTIL DEATH DO US...

Epitaphs of loving (and not so loving) spouses

i fear
no fate (for you are my fate, my sweet)
i want no world (for beautiful you are my world, my true)
and it's you are whatever a moon has always meant
and whatever a sun will always sing is you
i carry your heart (i carry it in my heart)

Ellion Jon Barrens

FOREST LAWN CEMETERY
HOLLYWOOD HILLS, LOS ANGELES

Excerpted from the poem, "i carry your heart with me," by e.e. cummings.

Sacred to the memory of Anthony Drake
Who died for peace and quietness sake
His wife was constantly scolding and scoffin'
So he sought for repose in a twelve-dollar coffin

Anthony Drake

BURLINGTON CHURCHYARD,
MASSACHUSETTS

I plant these shrubs upon your grave dear wife
That something in this spot may boast of life
Shrubs may wither and all earth rot
Shrubs may revive, but you, thank heaven
Will not

Anonymous

RHAGADER, WALES

Sacred to the memory of Elisha Philbrook
and his wife Sarah
Beneath these stones do lie
Back to back, my wife and I!
When the last trumpet the air shall fill
If she gets up, I'll just lie still

Elisha Philbrook

SARGENTVILLE, MAINE

Sacred to the memory of Jared Bates
Who died Aug. the 6th, 1800
His widow, aged 24, lives at 7 Elm Street
Has every qualification for a good wife
And longs to be comforted

Jared Bates

LINCOLN, MAINE
1800

Here lies my wife in earthy mould
When she lived did naught but scold
Good friends go softly in your walking
Lest she should wake and rise up talking

Anonymous

1694

36-33-01-24-17

Honey you don't know what you did for me,
always playing the lottery.
The numbers you picked came in to play,
two days after you passed away.
For this, a huge monument I do erect,
for now I get a yearly check.
How I wish you were alive,
for now we are worth 8.5

Elizabeth Rich

EUFAULA HISTORICAL CEMETERY
EUFAULA, ALABAMA

Here lies my wife! Here let her lie!
Now she's at rest and so am I

Epitaph intended for the wife of
English poet John Dryden
(1631–1700)

Here lyes MARY the Wife of JOHN FORD
We hope her soul is gone to the LORD
But if for Hell she has chang'd this life
She had better be there than be John Ford's wife

Mary Ford

POTTERNE, WILTSHIRE
ENGLAND
1790

The children of Israel wanted bread
And the Lord gave them manna
Old clerk Wallace wanted a wife
And the Devil sent him Anna

Anna Wallace

ST. LEONARD'S CHURCH
RIBBESFORD, ENGLAND
19th century, composed by her husband, the parish clerk.

Beneath this stone
Lie Humphrey and Joan
Who rest together in peace
Living indeed
They disagreed
But now all quarrels cease

Anonymous

Here Lies Jane Smith
Wife of Thomas Smith
Marble Cutter:
This Monument Erected
By Her Husband
As A Tribute
To Her Memory.
Monuments of this style
are 250 Dollars

Jane Smith

A 19th-century epitaph-cum-billboard, composed by Thomas Smith for his wife. Believed to be in Annapolis.

To the four husbands of
Miss Ivy Saunders
1790, 1794, 1808, 18??
Here lie my husbands,
One, Two, Three
Dumb as men could ever be.
As for my Fourth, well, praise be to God,
He bides for a little above the sod.
Alex, Ben, Sandy were the first threes' names,
And to make things tidy, I'll add his – James

Ivy Saunders

SHUTESBURG, MASSACHUSETTS

Here Lieth The Body Of
My Lovely Dear Wife Anne
Who Plays The Poker Machines
Whenever She Can

Anne Hewitt

HELENSBURGH CEMETERY
NEW SOUTH WALES, AUSTRALIA

Epitaph composed by James Thomas Hewitt, for whom the following was later added:

Here Lie The Bones
They Call Him Uncle Jim
He Sits Here And Drinks
While She Puts His Money In

2 better wives
1 man never had
They were gifts from God
But are now in Heaven
May God help me
So to meet them there
Reader! Meet us in heaven

Henrietta and Susanna Bean

WELLESLEY TOWNSHIP
ONTARIO, CANADA
1867

This epitaph is actually decoded from the original stone created by Samuel Bean, which featured a seemingly random array of letters, 15 across and 15 down. Readers were invited to solve the puzzle. But no one did until 1947, when it was first deciphered by the cemetery's caretaker, John Hammond.

II

Celebrity Goodbyes

Messages from the stars above (or wherever)

Gracie Allen
1902–1964

George Burns
1896–1996

Together again

Inscription on crypt in Forest Lawn cemetery, Glendale, CA, shared by legendary vaudevillians Burns and Allen. It is said that Burns visited his late wife's grave every month for the 32 years by which he outlived her.

No Man Is Indispensable But Some Are Irreplaceable

Wallace Beery

BEVERLY HILLS, CALIFORNIA
1949

Beery was a film actor whose credits include The Champ (1931, with Jackie Cooper), which won an Academy Award.

A star on earth –
A star in heaven

Karen Carpenter

CYPRESS, CALIFORNIA
1983

American pop singer who, with her brother Richard, recorded 23 hit singles (including "We've Only Just Begun") and sold over 80 million albums. She died from cardiac arrest brought on by a persistent eating disorder. She was only 32.

That's All Folks

Mel Blanc

HOLLYWOOD, CALIFORNIA
1989

Epitaph taken from the line that ended all Warner Brothers cartoons, featuring characters made famous with Blanc's voice, including Bugs Bunny, Daffy Duck, Porky Pig, Sylvester the Cat, and Tweety Bird.

Sleep with a smile

Sammy Cahn

HOLLYWOOD, CALIFORNIA
1993

Born Samuel Cohen in 1913, American lyricist collaborated on many popular songs in the 1940s, 1950s and 1960s, including the Frank Sinatra hit, "Come Fly With Me."

She did it the hard way

Bette Davis

HOLLYWOOD, CALIFORNIA
1989

American film star with over 100 features to her credit, including two Academy Awards for best actress. The "hard way" may have referred to her four marriages, health problems, or conflicts with other stars, notably Joan Crawford.

The Entertainer:
He did it all

Sammy Davis Jr.

HOLLYWOOD, CALIFORNIA
1990

Versatile performer who began in vaudeville at the age of two, and went on to make movies, recordings and live performances.

Good night, Sweet Prince
And a flight of angels sing to thy rest

Douglas Fairbanks Sr.

HOLLYWOOD, CALIFORNIA
1939

Swashbuckling film actor of the 1920s. His epitaph, borrowed from Shakespeare's Hamlet, *also appears on the gravestones of actors John Barrymore and Tyrone Power.*

He made us laugh
He took my pain away
I love you
Lauretta

Marty Feldman

HOLLYWOOD, CALIFORNIA
1982

Comic British actor and writer who died of a heart attack following a severe case of food poisoning. His epitaph was composed by Lauretta, his wife of 23 years.

A genius of comedy
His talent brought joy and
Laughter to all the world

Oliver Hardy

NORTH HOLLYWOOD, CALIFORNIA
1957

Comic actor who teamed with Stan Laurel to make a string of films that reached their peak of popularity in the 1930s. Remarkably agile for a man weighing in at over 300 pounds, his physical style of comedy was unmatched.

A Master of Comedy His Genius In The Art of Humor Brought Gladness To The World He Loved

Stan Laurel

HOLLYWOOD HILLS, CALIFORNIA
1965

Born Arthur Stanley Jefferson in England, Laurel came to America and teamed with Oliver Hardy to create the most successful comedy duo of his generation. Reported to have told his friends: "If any of you cry at my funeral, I'll never speak to you again."

Beloved Mother
Oct. 17, 1918 – May 14, 1987
To Yesterday's Companionship and Tomorrow's Reunion

Rita Hayworth

HOLY CROSS CEMETERY
CULVER CITY, CALIFORNIA
1987

Born Margarita Carmen Cansino, became screen siren Rita Hayworth (adopting her mother's maiden name) during the 1940s, and a popular pin-up girl for American soldiers in World War II. Mother of two daughters, one by noted actor Orson Welles.

Everybody Loves Somebody Sometime

Dean Martin

LOS ANGELES, CALIFORNIA
1995

Epitaph is taken from one of Martin's most popular songs, which was also the musical theme for his 1970s television program, The Dean Martin Show.

The Best Is Yet To Come

Frank Sinatra

PALM SPRINGS, CALIFORNIA
1998

Widely considered to be one of the best song stylists of all time, Sinatra's epitaph is taken from one of his biggest hits. It may be particularly appropriate to his heirs: royalties from Sinatra's music are now reported to exceed $6 million annually.

Thank you for all the love you gave me
There could be no one stronger
Thank you for the many beautiful songs
They will live long and longer

Hank Williams, Sr.

OAKWOOD CEMETERY
MONTGOMERY, ALABAMA
1953

A legend of traditional country music, Williams' songs were almost certain to live longer than he did. An extraordinary consumer of drugs and alcohol, he died at the age of only 29.

I never met a man I didn't like

Will Rogers

CLAREMORE, OKLAHOMA
1935

Cowboy, columnist, actor and broadcaster, Rogers was famous for his simple humanity. His epitaph is one of his most famous sayings.

One of a kind

Buddy Rich

WESTWOOD MEMORIAL PARK
LOS ANGELES, CALIFORNIA
1987

Widely considered to be one of the world's great jazz drummers, Rich was never one to mince words.

Go away. I'm asleep

Joan Hackett

HOLLYWOOD, CALIFORNIA
1983

Before her premature death at the age of 49, Ms Hackett appeared in a number of television and film productions, including "The Terminal Man" (1979) and "Only When I Laugh" (1981). She believed in getting her beauty sleep – as her epitaph reminds us.

Κατα τον δαιμονα εαυ του
(***Kata ton daimona eau tou*** – **True to his own spirit**)

Jim Morrison

PÈRE LACHAISE CEMETERY
PARIS, FRANCE
1971

Since his "death by misadventure" in Paris, the gravesite of Morrison, lead singer of The Doors, remains one of that city's top tourist destinations.

III

They Had It Coming

Of rustlers, reprobates, gunfighters, and card players

Shed not for her a bitter tear
Nor give the heart to vain regret
'Tis but the casket that lies here
The gem that filled it sparkles yet

Belle Starr

Infamous "Bandit Queen" of the Old West, shot in 1889, at the age of 40, by an unknown assailant. Buried at Younger's Bend, about 70 miles southwest of Fort Smith, Arkansas.

He looked for gold
And died of lead poison

Anonymous gold-digger

Here lies young Ezikel Height
Died from jumping Jim Smith's claim
Didn't happen at the mining site
The claim he jumped was Jim Smith's dame

Ezikel Height

Played five aces
Now he's playing the harp

Unknown (and rather careless) gambler

BOOT HILL CEMETERY

Here lies Butch
We planted him raw
He was quick on the trigger
But slow on the draw

Butch

Silver City, Nevada
circa 1862

It is believed that "Butch" was actually one John Pearse, a part-time gunfighter and full-time drunk.

...that nothing's so sacred as honor
and nothing's so loyal as love

Wyatt Earp

Hills of Eternity
Colma, California
1929

Best known for his role in the legendary gunfight at the OK Corral, Earp seemed almost certain to meet a violent end. Yet he retired to California, where he died peacefully in his bed at the age of 81.

Here lies the body of Thomas Kemp
Who lived by wool and died by hemp
There nothing would suffice the glutton
But with the fleece to steal the mutton
Had he but worked and lived uprighter
He'd ne'er been hung for a sheep-biter

Thomas Kemp

BLETCHLEY, BUCKS
ENGLAND

Kemp was a sheep rustler who was finally caught and hanged.

Here lies Sheriff Tim McGrew
Who said he would arrest Bill Hennessy or die
He was right

Sheriff Tim McGrew

TOPEKA, KANSAS

Here lies Slip McVey
He would be here today
But bad whiskey and a fast gun
Put him away

Slip McVey

PIOCHE, NEVADA

Here lies Lester Moore
Four slugs
From a 44
No Les
No more

Lester Moore

BOOTHILL GRAVEYARD
TOMBSTONE, ARIZONA
1880

Epitaph of a Wells Fargo agent who ran afoul of some outlaw.

Here lies John Timothy Snow
who died fighting for a lady's honor
(She wanted to keep it)

John Timothy Snow

BOOTHILL GRAVEYARD
TOMBSTONE, ARIZONA

Two things I love most,
Good horses and beautiful women
And when I die I hope they
Tan this old hide of mine
And make it into a ladies' riding saddle
So I can rest in peace between
The two things I love most

Russell J. Larsen

LOGAN, UTAH

Shot in the back
By a dirty rat

Charles Thompson

NANAIMO, B.C.
CANADA
1891

He called Bill Smith a liar

Anonymous

CRIPPLE CREEK, COLORADO

Toothless Nell
Killed 1876
In a dance brawl
Her last words:
"Circumstances led me to this end."

Alice Chambers
a.k.a. Toothless Nell

BOOT HILL CEMETERY
DODGE CITY
1878

At one time, Chambers had the dubious distinction of being the only woman buried in the notorious Boot Hill Cemetery.

Here lies Rab McBeth
Who died for the want of
Another breath

Rab McBeth

LARNE, IRELAND
1823

The breath referred to here was cut off by a noose.

Here under the dung of the cows and sheep
Lies an old highclimber fast asleep
His trees all topped and his lines all hung
They say the old rascal died full of rum

Paul Lennis Swank

CANYONVILLE, OREGON

"Highclimbers" were what we now call loggers or lumberjacks.

IV

Too Young to Die

Remembrances of lives only just begun

Sleep on sweet babe and take thy rest
God called thee home
For He thought it best

This simple epitaph has been used on hundreds, if not thousands, of infants' gravestones.

Nip't in the bud to blossom in heaven

Cora D. Hainer, died Oct. 25, 1888
in her 3rd year
James W. Hainer, died Sept. 27, 1888
in his 5th year

GUYSBORO CEMETERY
ELGIN COUNTY
ONTARIO, CANADA

Ope'd my eyes
Took a peep
Didn't like it
Went back to sleep

Gravestone of a newborn

ASHBY DE LA ZOOCH, ENGLAND
1949

Thy gentle voice now is hushed
Thy warm true heart is still
And on thy young and innocent brow
Is resting death's cold chill

William J. Bush, died May 1, 1896
in his fourth year

BALTIMORE, MARYLAND

Beneath this stone our baby lays
He neither cries nor hollers
He lived just one and twenty days
And cost us forty dollars

Infant's gravestone

BURLINGTON, VERMONT

Happy infant, early blest
Rest in peaceful slumber, rest

Caroline DeRidder, died April 22, 1840
aged 3 years

GREENWICH, NEW YORK

This epitaph was widely used for young children during the Victorian era, but rarely appears now.

Here lie two children
By water confounded
One died of dropsy
T'other was drownded

Anonymous epitaph for two infants

SUSSEX, ENGLAND

Weep not for me mother & brothers dear
It is God's wish that I am here
At my sweet age I swallowed a bone
That sent me to a happy home

William Henery

STAWELL CEMETERY
VICTORIA, AUSTRALIA

V

COULDN'T RESIST A PUN

Graveyard groaners

No hits, no runs, no heirs

Anonymous spinster

SCRANTON, PENNSYLVANIA

He angled in the babbling brook
With all his angler's skill
He lied about the fish he took
And here he's lying still

Anonymous fisherman

NEW YORK

Stranger, tread this ground with gravity
Dentist Brown is filling his last cavity

Anonymous dentist

St. George's Cemetery
Edinburgh, Scotland

Whenever patients come to I,
I physics, bleeds, and sweats 'em
If after that they choose to die,
What's that to me! – I letts 'em

John Coakley Lettsom

1744–1815

Reputedly written by the poet Thomas Erskine, this epitaph combines a fairly accurate picture of 18th-century medical treatments with a rather bad pun on the name of Dr. Lettsom, a noted Quaker physician and founding member of the Medical Society of London, who was known to sign his prescriptions, "I Lettsom."

Under the sod and under the trees
Lies the body of Jonathan Pease
He is not here, there's only the pod
Pease shelled out and went to God

Jonathan Pease

NANTUCKET, MASSACHUSETTS
CIRCA 1880

Under this sod
Lies another

Anonymous

This epitaph, probably apocryphal, is typically better understood by those from Britain, where "sod" also means "bugger."

Here lie I bereft of breath
Because a cough carried me off
Then a coffin carried me off in

Anonymous

GRANARY BURYING GROUND
BOSTON, MASSACHUSETTS

On the 22nd of June
Jonathan Fiddle
Went out of tune

Jonathan Fiddle

HARTSCOMBE, ENGLAND

Here lies Ann Mann
She lived an old maid and
She died an Old Mann

Ann Mann

BATH ABBEY, ENGLAND
1767

In memory of Lettice Manning,
who died 11th July 1757, aged 19 years
Oh! cruel death, to please thy palate
Cut down Lettice to make a sallet

ST. PETER'S CHURCHYARD
MOULTON, ENGLAND

This epitaph makes a couple of grisly puns. "Sallet" is an old word for salad.

Reader if cash thou art
In want of any
Dig 4 feet deep
And thou wilt find a Penny

John Penny

WIMBORNE, ENGLAND

Here lieth W.W.
Who never more will
Trouble you
Trouble you

William Wilson

LONDON, ENGLAND

Literary Lions

Last words from those who were famous for them

Cosmos Mariner
Destination Unknown

Conrad Aiken

BONAVENTURE CEMETERY
SAVANNAH, GEORGIA
1973

The origin of this epitaph is reportedly that Aiken, a Southern poet, enjoyed watching ships come and go in Savannah, and one day saw a ship called the Cosmos Mariner. Intrigued by the name (many of his poems refer to the cosmos), he looked it up in the shipping news, which listed it as "destination unknown." He thought this most appropriate to the ship's name – and to his gravestone (bench-shaped, to accommodate other ship watchers).

Sleep after toyle
Port after stormie seas
Ease after warre
Death after life
Does greatly please

Joseph Conrad

CANTERBURY, ENGLAND
1924

Conrad was the author of a number of books, including Heart of Darkness *(upon which the film* Apocalypse Now *was based). His epitaph is taken from Spenser's "The Faerie Queene."*

The passive master lent his hand
To the vast Soul which o'er him planned

Ralph Waldo Emerson

SLEEPY HOLLOW CEMETERY
CONCORD, MASSACHUSETTS
1882

Emerson's final resting place is nearby a number of famous American authors, including Henry Thoreau (1862) and Nathaniel Hawthorne (1864). The epitaph above is taken from one of his own poems, "The Problem."

Emily Dickinson
Born
Dec. 10, 1830
Called Back
May 15, 1886

Emily Dickinson

WEST CEMETERY
AMHERST, MASSACHUSETTS

Although largely unrecognized while she was alive, Dickinson is now considered one of America's finest poets.

So we beat on, boats against the current
Borne back ceaselessly into the past

Francis Scott Key (F. Scott) Fitzgerald

ROCKVILLE, MARYLAND
1940

Fitzgerald, a noted American novelist (author of The Great Gatsby, *from which the epitaph is taken) and screenwriter, is buried with his wife, Zelda, who died in 1948, in a fire at the mental institution in which she had been confined.*

Steel True, Blade Straight

Arthur Conan Doyle

MINSTEAD CHURCHYARD
HAMPSHIRE, ENGLAND
1930

Doyle was best known as the creator of Sherlock Holmes, although writing was just one of his many accomplishments, including those as a physician and sportsman. His epitaph is a reflection of the Victorian spirit of determination and honor.

I Had a Lover's Quarrel with the World

Robert Frost

BENNINGTON, VERMONT
1963

One of America's greatest poets, Frost is buried next to his wife, Elinor, who predeceased him in 1938. Her epitaph: "Together Wing to Wing and Oar to Oar."

Men must endure their going hence

C.S. Lewis

HEADINGTON QUARRY CHURCHYARD
OXFORD, ENGLAND
1963

Epitaph taken from the final act of Shakespeare's King Lear.

The Stone The Builders Rejected

Jack London

JACK LONDON STATE HISTORIC PARK
GLEN ELLEN, CALIFORNIA
1916

London wrote a remarkable 51 books and 191 short stories before he died at the age of 40.

Gone are the living but the dead remain
And not neglected, for a hand unseen
Scattering its bounty like a summer rain
Still keeps their graves and their remembrance green

Henry Wadsworth Longfellow

Mount Auburn Cemetery
Cambridge, Massachusetts
1882

Epitaph taken from Longfellow's poem, "The Jewish Cemetery at Newport."

Quoth the raven
"Nevermore"

Edgar Allan Poe

Baltimore, Maryland
1849

Poe died at the age of only 40, ill and destitute. It was not until 26 years after Poe's death that a group of schoolchildren raised money to erect the gravestone that now bears his epitaph, taken from perhaps his most famous poem, "The Raven."

Good friend for Jesus sake forbeare
To dig the dust encloased heare!
Blest be the man that spares these stones
And curst be he that moves my bones

William Shakespeare

HOLY TRINITY CHURCH
STRATFORD-UPON-AVON, ENGLAND
1616

Shakespeare composed this epitaph, apparently as a simple warning to leave his remains alone. He died of unknown causes at the age of 52.

Against you I will fling myself
Unvanquished and unyielding, O Death!

Virginia Woolf

RODMELL, SUSSEX
1941

Woolf's epitaph was selected by her husband, Leonard, after she committed suicide by drowning. It was taken from her novel, The Waves.

Life is a jest and all things show it
I thought so once and now I know it

John Gay

WESTMINSTER ABBEY
1732

Gay was a dramatist, probably best known for "The Beggar's Opera."

If after I depart this vale
You ever remember me
And have thought
To please my ghost
Forgive some sinner and
Wink your eye at some homely girl

H.L. Mencken

LOUDON PARK CEMETERY
BALTIMORE, MARYLAND
1956

Mencken was a leading American journalist, editor, and critic.

Here beneath rest the ashes of a man
Who was in the habit of postponing
Everything 'till the day after.
However, at last, he improved and really
Died January 31, 1972

Fritiof Nilsson Piraten

SIMRISHAMN
SKANE LAN, SWEDEN

One of Sweden's best-known writers, Piraten was also clearly something of a procrastinator.

VII

Cautionary Verses

Lessons in living from those who no longer are

Ma loved Pa
Pa loved women
Ma caught Pa with one in swimming
Here lies Pa

Anonymous grave in Florida

Looked up the elevator shaft
To see if the car was on the way down.
It was

Harry Edsel Smith

ALBANY, NEW YORK
1942

I've made a lot of deals in my lifetime
But I went in the hole on this one

Anonymous

Baton Rouge, Louisiana

Grim death took me
Without any warning
I was well at night
And dead in the morning

Anonymous

Sevenoaks Churchyard
Kent, England

Here lies an atheist
All dressed up
And no place to go

Atheist unknown

THURMONT, MARYLAND

Here lies a miser who lived for himself
Who cared for nothing but gathering wealth
Now where he is and how he fares
Nobody knows and nobody cares

Miser unknown

LEAMINGTON, ENGLAND

I thought it was a mushroom when
I found it in the woods forsaken
But since I sleep beneath this mound
I must have been mistaken

Anonymous

CLEVELAND, OHIO

Stop, reader, pray, and read my fate
What caused my life to terminate
For thews by night when in my bed
Brook up my house and shot me dead

William Mansbridge of Cadnam

CHURCH OF ST. MARY
ELING HILL, ENGLAND
1703

"Thews" are thieves; "brook" means "broke."

Where e'er you be
Let your wind go free
Keeping it in
Was the death of me

Anonymous

NORWOOD
LONDON, ENGLAND

Variations on this epitaph (and its advice) also appear in Australia and a number of other countries with an appreciation for flatulent humor.

Here lies the body
of Jonathan Blake
Who stepped on the gas
Instead of the brake

Jonathan Blake

UNIONTOWN, PENNSYLVANIA

She always said her feet were killing her
But nobody believed her

Margaret Daniels

Hollywood Cemetery
Richmond, Virginia

Beneath this stone
A lump of clay
Lies Uncle Peter Daniels
Who too early in the
month of May
Took off his winter flannels

Peter Daniels

Medway, Massachusetts
1746

Here lies George Hill
Who from a cliff
Fell quite stiff
When it happen'd is not known
Therefore not mentioned on this stone

George Hill

St. Peter's Churchyard
Isle of Thanet, England

Here lies Matthew
Hollingshead
Who died from cold
Caught in his head
It brought on fever and
rheumatiz
Which ended me
For here I is

Matthew Hollingshead

Northumberland, England

Here lies the body of our Anna
Done to death by a banana
It wasn't the fruit that laid her low
But the skin of the thing
That made her go

Anna Hopewell

ENOSBURG FALLS, VERMONT

Here lies the body of Mary Ann Lowder
She burst while drinking a Seidlitz powder
Called from this world to her heavenly rest
She should have waited till it effervesced

Mary Ann Lowder

BURLINGTON, VERMONT

Seidlitz powder was the forerunner of Alka Seltzer, and was a popular "morning after" remedy throughout the 19th and early 20th centuries.

Erected to the memory of John Philips
Accidentally shot as a mark
Of affection by his brother

John Philips

SARATOGA, NEW YORK

Ellen Shannon
Fatally burned March 21, 1870
By the explosion of a lamp
Filled with
"R. E. Danforth's Non-Explosive Burning Fluid"

Ellen Shannon

GIRARD, PENNSYLVANIA

Sarah Shute
1803–1840
Here lies, cut down like unripe fruit
The wife of Deacon Amos Shute
She died of drinking too much coffee
Anno Dominy eighteen forty

Sarah Shute

CANAAN, NEW HAMPSHIRE

All you that read with little care
Who walk away and leave me here
Should not forget that you must die
And be entombed as well as I

Hannal Collins

DORSET CEMETERY, VERMONT
1791

Death is a debt to nature due
Which I have paid and so will you

Isaac Kibbe

ENFIELD, CONNECTICUT
1766

One-Liners

Where brevity is the soul of wit (and saves on engravers' fees)

The defense rests

John E. Goembel, Attorney

WILLWOOD CEMETERY
ROCKFORD, ILLINOIS
1946

This is also recorded as being suggested by British lawyer and author John Mortimer ("Rumpole of the Bailey" and others), as his epitaph.

Dr. Fred Roberts
1875–1931
Office upstairs

Fred Roberts, MD

BROOKLAND, ARKANSAS

She sleeps alone at last

Anonymous (and notorious) actress

Epitaph composed by US humorist Robert Benchley (1889-1945).

A victim of fast women and slow horses

Milt MacPhail

TECK TWP. CEMETERY
KIRKLAND LAKE, ONTARIO
1985

No flowers please. I'm allergic

Goodman Ace

RAYTOWN, MISSOURI
1982

Comic writer and performer, known for the radio program "Easy Aces" (also featuring his wife) which aired in the 1930s and 1940s.

Big deal! I'm used to dust

Erma Bombeck

DAYTON, OHIO
1996

Renowned newspaper columnist and humorist, Bombeck is buried under a large boulder, shipped in from her home in Arizona.

Excuse my dust

Dorothy Parker

DIED AND CREMATED 1967
ASHES INTERRED
NAACP HEADQUARTERS
BALTIMORE, MARYLAND
1988

Noted humorist and writer Dorothy Parker suggested this epitaph, but it was never inscribed as such. Instead, her suggestion was noted as part of a longer memorial plaque marking where her ashes were finally interred after having sat on various shelves for 21 years.

Getting there is half the fun!

Samuel J. McKelvey

MOUNT PLEASANT CEMETERY
TORONTO, CANADA

A fitting epitaph, since McKelvey was a director of tourism for the Canadian government.

I told you I was sick

William H. Hahn, Jr.

PRINCETON, NEW JERSEY
1980

This epitaph is widely known, but is rarely attributed to anyone in particular. (Typical references are "from a cemetery in Georgia" or something similar.) Here, the epitaph, and the person, is (and was) real.

I made an ash out of myself

Julian Skaggs

WEST VIRGINIA

I Don't Want To Talk About It Now

Bonnie Anderson

FOREST LAWN CEMETERY
LOS ANGELES, CALIFORNIA

Transplanted

Lorenzo Sabine

HILLSIDE CEMETERY
EASTPORT, MAINE
1877

Sabine was a congressman for Massachusetts.

IX

Worthy Remembrances

Memorable epitaphs from all kinds of people

I'll see you in apple blossom time

Thomas P. "Tip" O'Neill

MOUNT PLEASANT CEMETERY
HARWICH, MASSACHUSETTS

O'Neill served for many years as Speaker of the US House of Representatives. He died in 1994 at the age of 81. His epitaph is from the title of a 1941 song made famous by the Andrews Sisters.

This one is on me

Dr. William Rothwell

PAWTUCKET, RHODE ISLAND
1942

This epitaph, inscribed on a larger boulder, memorializes a generous New England physician who had a reputation for always picking up the bill.

The body of
B. Franklin, Printer
Like the cover of an old book
Its contents worn out
And stript of its lettering and gilding
Lies here, food for worms.
Yet the work itself shall not be lost
For it will, as he believed
Appear once more
In a new and more beautiful edition
Corrected and amended
By the Author

Benjamin Franklin

CHRIST CHURCH CEMETERY
PHILADELPHIA, PENNSYLVANIA
1790

Vocatus Atque
Non Vocatus
Deus Aderit
(Called or Not Called, God will be present)

Carl Jung

KUSNACHT, SWITZERLAND
1961

This epitaph, from one of the 20th century's most influential psychiatrists, was inscribed over the doorway to his home and, ultimately, on his gravestone.

School is out
Teacher
Has gone home

S.B. McCracken

ELKHART, INDIANA

Epitaph composed by McCracken, a school teacher and principal.

...If I take the wings of the morning and dwell in the uttermost part of the sea...

Charles Lindbergh

KIPAHULU, HAWAII
1974

Pioneering aviator Lindbergh's epitaph is taken from Psalm 139. The line that follows it is: "even there shall thy hand lead me..."

She thought of others ever
Herself never
We can't forget

Melinda "Minnie" Pike

EVERGREEN CEMETERY
AROOSTOOK, MAINE
1923

If cannibals should ever catch me
I hope they will say
"We have eaten Dr. Schweitzer
He was good to the end
And the end wasn't bad"

Albert Schweitzer

ALBERT SCHWEITZER HOSPITAL
LAMBARENE, GABON
AFRICA
1965

This Nobel Peace prizewinner's grave is a simple cross with his name and dates inscribed in French. His epitaph is reportedly the one he had suggested for himself.

Few hearts like his, with virtue warm'd
Few heads with knowledge so inform'd
If there's another world he lives in bliss
If there is none he made the best of this

William Muir

1793
Epitaph composed by a friend of Muir's, Scottish poet Robert Burns. The poem has been quoted in numerous epitaphs since.

I Am Woman
Hear Me Roar
And Boy Did She

Anonymous

DOUGLAS COUNTY, NEBRASKA

None knew thee but to love thee
Nor named thee but to praise

Joseph Rodman Drake

BRONX COUNTY, NEW YORK
1820

Taken from the poem, "On the Death of Joseph Rodman Drake" (1795-1820), by Fitz-Greene Halleck (1790-1867). These lines were widely used on gravestones throughout the Victorian era.

I had it all
I did it all
I loved it all

Sid Luckman

SKOKIE, ILLINOIS
1998

Luckman was a football hall-of-famer for the Chicago Bears in the 1940s.

Afflictions sore long have I bore
Physicians were in Vain
Till God said please my grief to ease
And free from my pain

Thomas Bruce

LIBERTY CHURCH CEMETERY
LIBERTY TOWNSHIP, OHIO
1883

Hi!
Stay high
Bye

Anonymous

GRAVESTONE FEATURING ENGRAVED
MARIJUANA LEAF
HOOKSTOWN, PENNSYLVANIA

My trip is ended
Send my samples home

Thomas W. Campbell

BURLINGTON, IOWA

Campbell was a travelling salesman.

In loving remembrance
Died April 29, 1904
Aged
30,686
days old

William Nicholls

UXBRIDGE, ONTARIO
CANADA

A native of Cornwall, England, Nicholls took lifelong pride in always being able to say how many days old he was.

Here I lie at the Chancel Door
Here I lie because I am poor
The farther in the more they pay
But here lie I as warm as they

Thomas Docton

HARTLAND CHURCH
DEVON, ENGLAND
CIRCA 1600

In the 17th century, it was common practice to bury the dead under the floor of the church. The richer you were (or the more "pit money" you could afford to pay), the closer you were located to the altar. The poor were consigned to the churchyard outside. As we can see from this epitaph, those who were of modest means ended up somewhere in between.

When I am dead and in my grave
And all my bones are rotten
While reading this you'll think of me
When I am long forgotten

Anonymous

ST. JAMES CATHEDRAL
TORONTO, CANADA

This epitaph was widely used throughout North America in the 18th and 19th centuries, often in conjunction with other verses. The rhyme was also popular for use in samplers and other memorabilia.

X

Fractured Farewells

Epitaphs for which the dearly departed might not be eternally grateful

In this grave ye see before ye
Lyes berried up a dismal story
A young maiden crossed in love
And tooketh to the realms above
But he that crossed her I should say
Deserves to go the other way

Anonymous

PENTEWAN, CORNWALL
ENGLAND

"Amazing"

In the eighteenth and nineteenth centuries, children were often given names that are rarely heard now – names such as Prudence, Charity, Faith, and so on. One boy was named Amazing – which, even by the standard of the day, was cause for some amusement. Not surprisingly, the boy came to hate his name.

When he grew old, after a lifetime of jokes, he told his wife that when the time came, he did not want his name on his tombstone. And so, when he died, she followed his wishes and put on the tombstone,

"Here lies a man who was faithful to his wife for 60 years."

Of course, this anonymous tribute did not allow the man to escape the curse of his name, since everyone who viewed the epitaph would invariably exclaim,

"Why, that's Amazing!"

By and by
God caught his eye

Epitaph for a waiter

Attributed to American poet David McCord, from Epitaphs: The Waiter. *A variant, "At last God caught his eye," is attributed to Welsh comedian Harry Secombe, in "Epitaph for a head waiter,"* Punch *(London, May 17, 1962).*

Here lies
Ezekial Aikle
Age 102
The Good Die Young

Ezekial Aikle

EAST DALHOUSIE CEMETERY
NOVA SCOTIA, CANADA

Here lies in a horizontal position
the outside case of Thomas Hinde
Clock and watch maker
Who departed this life wound up
In hope of being taken in hand
By his Maker and being
Thoroughly cleaned repaired and
Set a-going in the world to come.
On the 15th of August 1836
In the nineteenth year of his life

Thomas Hinde

BOLSOVER, ENGLAND
1836

Her name, cut clear upon this marble cross
Shines, as it shone when she was still on earth
While tenderly the mild, agreeable moss
Obscures the figures of her date of birth

Anonymous (and persistently vain) actress

Epitaph from a poem by sharp-tongued US writer Dorothy Parker (1893-1967).

Here lies the body of Margaret Bent
She kicked up her heels and
Away she went

Margaret Bent

WINTERBORN STEEPLETON CEMETERY
DORSETSHIRE, ENGLAND

This stone was raised to Sarah Ford
Not Sarah's virtues to record
For they're well known to all the town
No Lord; it was raised to keep her down

Sarah Ford

KILMURRY CHURCH
IRELAND

Down the lanes of memory
The lights are never dim
Until the stars forget to shine
We shall remember...her

Anonymous

Who says epitaphs have to rhyme?

Here lies the body of Martha Dias,
Who was always uneasy, and not over pious
She lived to the age of three score and ten
And gave that to the worms she refused to the men

Martha Dias

SHREWSBURY
SHROPSHIRE, ENGLAND
1828

Beneath this stone and not above it
Lies the remains of Anna Lovett
Be pleased good reader not to shove it
Least she should come again above it
For twixt you and I, no one does covet
To see again this Anna Lovett

Gravestone reportedly somewhere in England; exact location (or actual existence) is unknown.

Owen Moore
Gone away
Owin' more
Than he could pay

Owen Moore

BATTERSEA CEMETERY
LONDON, ENGLAND

At rest beneath this slab of stone
Lies stingy Jimmy Wyatt
He died one morning just at ten
And saved a dinner by it

Jimmy Wyatt

FALKIRK, ENGLAND

Here lies one Wood
Enclosed in wood
One Wood
Within another
The outer wood
Is very good
We cannot praise
The other

Beza Wood

WINSLOW, MAINE
1837

Remember friend as you walk by
As you are now so once was I
As I am now you will surely be
Prepare thyself to follow me

Anonymous

Variations on this epitaph have been used for centuries on gravestones throughout the world. Occasionally, passersby have added something like: "To follow you I'm not content/Until I know which way you went!"

Here lies Kelly
We buried him today
He lived the life of Riley
...When Riley was away!

Anonymous

OCONTO FALLS, WISCONSIN

Here lies
Suzannah Ensign
Lord she is thin*

Suzannah Ensign

COOPERSTOWN, NEW YORK

**Despite appearances, the cause of Ms Ensign's death was not, as far as we know, starvation. The story is that the stonemason ran out of room and omitted the final "e" of "thine."*

Here lies the landlord Tommy Dent
In his last cozy tenement

Tommy Dent

ST. STEPHEN CHURCHYARD
WEST PURFORD, ENGLAND

Here lies the bones, of Joseph Jones
Who ate whilst he was able
But once o'erfed, he drop't down dead
And fell beneath the table
When from the tomb, to meet his doom
He rises amidst sinners
Since he must dwell, in heav'n or hell
Take him – which gives best dinners

Joseph Jones

WOLVERHAMPTON, ENGLAND
1690

Reader pass on the ne'er waste your time
On bad biography and bitter rhyme
For what I am this crumb'rous clay insures
And what I was, is no affair of yours

Mary Lefavour

TOPSFIELD, MASSACHUSETTS
1797

Epitaph for a compiler of epitaphs...

Come...

where

always

it's

Spring and everyone's

in love and flowers pick themselves

Adapted from the poem, "who knows if the moon's," by e.e. cummings.